Copyright © 2014 by Daniel McKim
All rights reserved. This book or any portion thereof may not manner whatsoever without the express written permission of the author except for the use of brief quotations in a book review.

Title ID: 4841112
ISBN-13: 978-1499791129

BEFORE STARTING ANY EXERCISE OR NUTRITION PROGRAM, PLEASE, CONSULT YOUR DOCTOR. BY TRAINING WITHIN THIS PROGRAM, YOU REALIZE THE RISKS INVOLVED WITH WEIGHT TRAINING AT THIS INTENSITY.

BIO

Daniel McKim has always had a knack for throwing things – what started out as throwing fits and pity parties, has turned into throwing heavy things. As a 15-time National Track and Field Qualifier and All-American at Northwest Missouri State University, McKim first watched a wild sport on ESPN that later became a passion. He was first intrigued by this sport, the Scottish Highland Games, for the opportunity to throw heavy objects resembling medieval war weapons, but the chance to compete with some of the top strength athletes in the world is what's kept him in the sport for 10 years.

In 2007 he was the world's top ranked amateur and upon making the jump to the pro ranks, he's continued the success –2011 and 2013 World Champion, 2010-2013 US National Champion, two-time World Caber Champion, one World and one North American record in each of the Scottish hammers.

Argued as one of the greatest caber tossers in recent history and the best the United States has ever produced, McKim has gone from being a local amateur competitor to a highly sought after worldwide athlete, speaker and author. McKim resides in the Kansas City area with his wife, Natalie, and their five boys.

Certifications Passed: NSCA CSCS, NESTA, ACE

Athletes Trained or Programs Written: Scottish Highland Games, track and field, football, baseball, soccer, basketball

Actual results (over five years) from a University throws program that used principles from Behemoth:
11 NCAA All-Americans
2 National Runner ups
24 National Qualifiers

Daniel McKim Lifts:
Bench Press – 475
Hang Clean – 420
Back Squat – 540
Incline – 440
Strict Overhead Press – 285
Front Squat – 455
Hang Snatch – 341

Website: www.believethrower.com
Facebook: www.facebook.com/mckimdaniel
Twitter: @DanielMcKim
YouTube: mckimdaniel

TABLE OF CONTENTS

LURKING INSIDE …	4
YOU AREN'T A MATHEMATICIAN – DON'T LIFT LIKE ONE	7
NO DEADS? ISN'T IT THE MOST AMAZING LIFT IN THE HISTORY OF EVER?	9
FIVE DAYS A WEEK IS TRAINING SUICIDE … OR IS IT?	10
SCHEDULED TIME OFF, BUT NOT FOR VACATION	12
PROGRAMMING FOR PEAK PERFORMANCE	14
THREE PHASES: SINEWS, BRONZE, IRON	16
THE BEHEMOTH DIET & SUPPLEMENTS	18
TECHNIQUE, TRAINING GEAR AND GENERAL POINTS OF CONTENTION	21
A WORD FROM YOUR LOCAL D.A.R.E. ROLE MODEL	23
EXERCISE DESCRIPTIONS	24
ABS/CORE	24
CHEST	25
TRICEPS	26
CLEANS/SNATCHES	26
LEGS	28
BACK	30
BICEPS	31
SHOULDERS	32
TRUE VICTORY	34
BEHEMOTH WORKOUT CARDS	35

1

LURKING INSIDE ...

For some time now, people have asked me to write and outline my training program and what my normal week looks like. For years I've been tweaking my style and routine. Even after ten years competing in the Highland Games and years of track and field, I am changing things, trying to find how I can best remedy my weaknesses. This book does that – it outlines what I do. I'll be honest, it's not easy. I don't always feel great. This isn't the magic pill to make you throw further, jump higher or run faster, like virtually every other training program promises. I can lay it out for you and give you direction, but it comes down to you waking up early, sacrificing time spent elsewhere and putting the work in to get better; to be a behemoth.

My bio is in this book, so I won't bore you with the details on the titles I've won, records set, All-Americans trained in this program, certification tests passed, or what my lifts are. Trust that I've built this program through my personal experiences and countless hours in the gym. It wasn't until my freshmen year in college that I truly found my love for strength training. In high school I enjoyed being strong, but it took me losing the opportunity to train for me to truly fall in love with it.

After my freshmen year at Northwest Missouri State University I had hernia surgery and spent weeks resting and recovering. When it was taken from me is when I realized how much I loved and missed it. When something is taken from us is many times when we realize what we've taken for granted.

I returned to the weight room with a hunger unlike anything I had experienced in terms of my desire for iron. I grabbed the football team's workout and started getting after it. I grew and got strong. I loved it. As the years went on, I worked with a strength coach to build my program. It was great and that provided me with a base that I have been altering ever since. It's amazing to look back now and realize I was just trying and experimenting. I had no idea about how to build a successful program, but I didn't care. I just wanted to lift

Fast forward to today, and I'm much wiser about my programming and how it affects my sport. I just wish I had built Behemoth back then.

As I was considering a name for my program, I turned to the greatest training book ever written: the Bible. If you haven't picked up that book, please, let me know and I'll send you one. Better yet, you can download an app instantly and get in the Word. I turned to the book of Job. The book of Job is about a man who is struggling and going through a myriad of trials and tribulations. He never turns his back on God, but questions why he, a righteous man, was going through all these miserable things. In chapter 40, God describes to Job His power, as it is shown in the creatures He created. One of these that He describes is, "Behemoth."

> "Behold now, Behemoth, which I made as well as you; He eats grass like an ox. Behold now, his strength in his loins and his power in the muscles of his belly. He bends his tail like a cedar; the sinews of his thighs are knit together. His bones are tubes of bronze; his limbs are like bars of iron. He is the first of the ways of God; let his maker bring near his sword. Surely the mountains bring him food, and all the beasts of the field

play there. Under the lotus plants he lies down, in the covert of the reeds and the marsh. The lotus plants cover him with shade; the willows of the brook surround him. If a river rages, he is not alarmed; he is confident, though the Jordan rushes to his mouth. Can anyone capture him when he is on watch, with barbs can anyone pierce his nose?" Job 40:15-24 NASB

If that doesn't get your blood boiling, then there's something wrong with you. Most likely, Behemoth was a dinosaur ... a huge creature that had no equal in power and strength. Not a bad creature to liken ourselves to. God's power is shown in His creation. For me, I want God's power to be shown in me. I want people to see me as a product of God's grace, mercy and direction. "Behemoth" seems like a fitting title to my program. God has directed me the whole time in my training and I want the glory to go back to Him.

So, is "Behemoth" a perfect program for everyone? No. I'll repeat that. This program is not a blanket program for all athletes. This program is for those who wish to be, or already are, a Behemoth. Behemoth is built for strength athletes and those who want to train like one. These, in my mind, are athletes in this mold: shot putters, discus throwers, hammer throwers, Scottish Highland gamers, offensive and defensive linemen, linebackers, tight ends, first basemen, and catchers. This program isn't for soccer midfielders, point guards, receivers, defensive backs, pitchers, center fielders, swimmers, divers ... do I need to go on? I'm just being honest. This isn't for everyone, but not everyone has the same goals as you and I – to be a large, immovable object built for demolition.

This program is the product of years of tweaking and experimenting. It's built on the things I've learned through years of time with iron in my grasp. This book isn't the product of lab tests or journal research. No single coach built this for me, neither has a peer reviewed expert co-authored this for me. I've taken insight and knowledge from some very smart coaches, but there's not a one of them I believed 100% in their programming. Is that short-sighted of me? Probably. Is that even a bit prideful of me? Yes, it is. But, that's an aspect I believe that is important – trust and believe that your current programming is the best option for you at this time.

I'm a hunter and one of the most frustrating things about it is putting up a tree stand – finding the "perfect spot," is impossible. It never fails. I'll scout and plan and place my stand in an amazing spot. I'm jacked about the monster bucks that will walk right under me ... until I get in the stand and see the sun come up. I sit there as deer pop out of areas where I am not and then the see it – the perfect spot. "Wow! I need to move over there!" I'll say to myself. I've always read, and believe, that you have to trust in your stand site. You have to believe that your spot is lights out and that there's no better place to be in the woods than where you're at. If you don't believe that, then you'll spend more time moving and altering than you ever will hunting.

I'm asking you to do something hard. I'm asking you to trust this program. I'm asking you to give it a full cycle of training to determine what you think. If you can commit to me for just 14 weeks, you won't be disappointed with where you'll be. Honestly, I'd like to think I'm saving you a few years. I'm saving you all the time it took for me to tweak, experiment and try new things. All the years I've spent learning in the gym are summarized in this short book.

If I could go back to high school, this is the workout I'd give myself. I'd tell myself to trust this program. I'd tell myself to eat more and gain 20 pounds. I'd tell myself to squat more. I'd tell myself to quit basketball and throw indoor shot. I'd tell myself to fall in love with training and not wait until college. I'd tell myself that my beloved Chiefs and Royals will disappoint me for years to come. I'd tell myself a lot of things, but I'd laminate this work out and put it in my locker. I'd tell myself to hold on tight – to be ready for the road ahead. I'd tell myself that, deep down inside me, there lurks a Behemoth.

2

YOU AREN'T A MATHEMATICIAN – DON'T LIFT LIKE ONE

You'll notice this book lacks what many people feel is all too critical for a training program – percentages. My training style does not rely on percentages of each max lift. I simply do not believe percentages to be critical to a successful training program and, in all actuality; I believe they can hinder you. I was speaking with an industry leader on this, who shared some of my same thoughts on percentages. He agreed that it's problematic when athletes base their training on something they may only do four times a year. He actually felt that, for percentages to truly work for your programming, you'd have to measure yourself on an almost weekly basis. He showed me how, at his school, they monitor many of their athletes on a daily basis with some of the world's top technology that acts more like medical science than strength science – breaking down your variances and how well you are recovering.

So many external factors affect our training; from sleep to diet, stress to emotional well-being and weather or climate changes for other athletes. With Behemoth, I'm aiming to help you with that. While I can't supply you with the world's top medical measurements, I'm giving you freedom. With this program, you'll get out of it what you put in. Instead of percentages, train on feeling. Notice I said, "feeling" and not, "motivation." If you're not motivated, don't even begin to train this way. Since you purchased this book, I'm assuming you're motivated and want to improve. I expect you to hit the weights on a weekly basis with a specific goal in mind and a desire to achieve it. Now, are you going to have your bad days where you aren't feeling it and are run down? Sure, I'm not naïve – trust I've been there many times, myself. But, those days should be far and few between. You should be hungry. If I were to list out percentages for you, it should just be 100%. 100% effort and 100% of the weight you can do for each exercise. You don't want to finish your session thinking you could have given more. This isn't a feeling you'll like – it's horrible.

To me, the flaw in percentage based training is that it doesn't always account for your progress within the program. You aren't testing your max weekly, so the ability to lift at a true updated percentage becomes difficult. In a successful program you're making progress, right? You'd like to make it on a weekly basis, wouldn't you? Then why would you limit yourself by basing your workouts on a test you did weeks or months prior? As the weeks go on, you're making jumps and your new max is much higher than it was during your initial test. All too many times I've lifted at my percentages, only to have them be too easy for me. Or, pending a myriad of external influencers, those percentages can bury you (injury, rest, over-training, nutrition, stress, etc.).

So, where does that leave us with percentages? If you train on "feeling," then how will you know what weight to put on the bar! *insert sarcastic double-hand slap to the face, ala Home Alone *.
What happened to putting iron in your hands and moving as much of it as you can? What if, as an athlete, you have a different work capacity than the next athlete? I'm going to guess you do. Scratch that; I **know** you do. Your ability to hit your reps at 80% may be relatively easy, while you might struggle to hit your sets when working at 90% of your max. This has nothing to do

with your established max, but with your individual make up – too many athletes are limiting, or burying, themselves with such a focus on volume requests. Your capacity for higher reps, for example, may be vastly different than mine or a million other athletes. For years, coaches and athletes have relied on percentages to dictate what they do in the gym that day and how much they accomplished that day. In turn, if you meet your percentages or hit or prescribed numbers, you've had a good day. Is that how you really want to measure yourself, regardless of how hard your worked or how you feel afterwards? Trust me, on the field of competition, hitting a threshold isn't going to cut it. But, if you give 100% and fall short, you've got nothing to hang your head about. Throw a few PRs, play the game of your life, go 4-4 from the plate, dominate your opponent, but still lose … not a bad day when you know you came and battled.

A problem with percentage based training is that too many athletes think that their weight and effort levels should correspond. 65% of their max can sometimes mean 65% effort. Eliminate this problem. Give 100% effort. I'm a firm believer that your working sets should be a product of what you can do that day. Now, I understand the success of this school of thought relies heavily on the athlete to be driven and passionate. If you have a desire to grow and succeed, this isn't problematic. I trust that, if you're reading this book, you're at that level. You're a behemoth. You don't need a percentage chart to tell you what weights you need to hit and how hard you should work. Why not do your working sets at the most that you can?

So many people smarter than me have built programs this way and believe them to be the best for themselves and their athletes. That's fine. I understand and respect that. I just don't think percentages are the only way for continued growth and development in your programming. "Hitting your percentages," or "Finishing as prescribed" should not dictate your success for the day. Push to make improvements each and every week. Write down what you do each day, or make mental notes, and work to improve on that next week. You are, and will be, a product of the time you spend doing the hard things. Push your body now so you can enjoy the spoils of your victories later.

3

NO DEADS? ISN'T IT THE MOST AMAZING LIFT IN THE HISTORY OF EVER?

Undoubtedly, you've skimmed through the text of this book, but gone straight to the daily breakdown in the back. I get it. I'd do the same thing. Actually, I'm probably lucky if any of you are actually reading this and not just tearing out the workouts.

What you've noticed, now, is that my workouts lack what many feel is a core lift – the deadlift. The deadlift has been known as the, "true test of strength and manhood." While your level of "manhood" obtained is critical, wouldn't you agree you'd rather smack homeruns, win events, pancake a defender, lead the league in rebounds, or set school records? In what seems like recent years, the strength community has jumped all over the deadlift. I don't know if this is a product of the popularity of powerlifting or CrossFit, but it's now expected that any successful strength program has the deadlift as one of its pillars. Now, this isn't the consensus among the strength and conditioning coaches I speak with, but let's face it – powerlifting and strongmen programming is at an all-time high in popularity, and those are staple events for those sports. In terms of general strength athletes, like you, training for carryover into your sport, it's not needed.

Well, in Behemoth, you won't find any deadlifts, and there's a valid reason. The only sniff of deadlifts that you'll get is the occasional modified straight leg deadlift and Romanian Deadlifts (RDLs). This is simply for accessory work on the hamstrings and glutes and done at a relatively light weight. These are not a primary lifts, and nor should they be. I think these are a good addition for sport specific movements, like the 56 pound Weight Over Bar event in the Scottish Highland Games. Strong hamstrings and glutes are imperative for back health, and this type of accessory work will strengthen your posterior chain while not overloading it into injury.

So, there will be no grinding in Behemoth. No good-mornings masked as deadlifts. No convulsing and seizures trying to lock out a dead. I don't believe they provide anywhere near the benefit many strength athletes profess. The risk vs. reward in the deadlift is not worth it – too many injuries to be suffered with poor deadlift technique. Your time with iron can be limited by work, family, or school, and you don't have time to spend on things that won't readily help you on the field, in the ring, on the diamond, in the box, or on the court.

Whether you're throwing a caber, smashing a homerun, drive blocking a defender, tossing a shot put or any other behemoth act, it's not off the ground. Even linemen, while starting in a three-point stance, don't find themselves in a position for the dead to help them greatly. Really, it's more of a sprinter's stance, with the force applied in driving, hip extension and pressing. Your sport is spent in the power-position, so why not train as such?

A Behemoth needs to focus his/her time on squats, presses and, of course, Olympic variations. This is also why I don't build full cleans and snatches into my programming. I believe hang cleans and hang snatches remain two of the most important lifts for sport. A Behemoth's time is better spent training in, and the natural progression towards, the power position. Train for a strong power position, and you'll find yourself in a position of power.

4

FIVE DAYS A WEEK IS TRAINING SUICIDE … OR IS IT?

The secret is out. There's no hiding it. This program calls for training five days a week … what!? "That's suicide!" you say. Not really. The way I've built this, you can comfortably train all five days each week. Also, it seems athletes at any level, whether that be high school or post-collegiate, can find an hour and fifteen to thirty minutes each day. Where things get hairy is when you're trying to squeeze three workouts in a week that each take two hours or more for you to complete. In the game of recovery, I've found that the body struggles to achieve solid gains when the exertion wanes past an hour and a half. Ideally, I'd even cut that time down fifteen minutes. This program should take you no more than that each day – if you're getting past that, it means you need to alter a few things in your training sessions. 1) Quit talking to your training partner or others in the gym. 2) Pick up the pace. 3) Put your phone away, or, 4) get out. Go home. You've done enough.

Now that I've talked you off the cliff, look at the program again – it's not that brutal each day. Will you be tired? Yes. Sore? You better believe it. Can you still practice during the week? Of course. I break down the body parts and muscle groups to work each day. You can liken it to "bodybuilding" training, but man, does it work. You might even liken my workouts to an upper/lower split with a "beach lifting" day in the middle. That's fine, but it's more intelligent and planned than that, and we must accept that our lat and bicep work, while fun and makes us look good at the pool, are important accessories for our bigger lifts. The lats and biceps are crucial for the development of better pulls from the hang position, bench press, posterior shoulder mobility for your overhead lifts. This leads us to better throws, more powerful blocking, less shoulder risk when you're locked on a defender in the trenches, and greater arm acceleration on your swing. Plus, did I mention the confidence for the pool and beach already?

Many of these upper/lower splits don't account for pairing the muscle groups together, which I think is a critical piece to recovery on a daily and weekly level. Realistically, you're still getting much of the push/pull split that many coaches and athletes hold to dearly. I've done a split like this, as well, and I find it hard to recover and build from. The reason I couldn't recover from those variations is that I felt like I was overtraining my body groups instead of breaking them down into separate workouts.

That's why I've built what I have. In short, it's Monday – chest and tris, Tuesday – cleans and posterior legs, Wednesday – back and biceps, Thursday – shoulders, Friday – snatches and anterior legs. If you look at it like this, you don't like it. Admit it. It looks like something a gym rat would tear out of a magazine and bring to the gym with him. But, as you dive deeper into the phases, sets, core lifts, scheduled time off, and periodization, you realize it's a more complex strength training program than you previously had.

Another reason why I like to split the body parts is the very reason I don't like "total body" workouts. If your program is centered on total body work, how often can you truly work that way and recover? Two, maybe three times a week? That's why I've never liked workouts combining bench and squats, only to be followed up with incline and deadlifts the next. Where's the recovery? There's really not much going on. You are overtraining.

My body takes 48+ hours to recover for me to train that muscle group or movement again, and that's why I love training five days a week. By breaking up the muscle groups and movements, you can train five days a week. Your body will grow and develop with volume – the key is to stimulate it with the right volume of lifts, without overtraining the body groups. Training five days a week isn't the ultimate goal; the goal is to be better at your sport. Let's do that. Let's be better at your sport. Let's get stronger, faster, more explosive, and more intense. Let's take your body to new levels. The weight room is your training ground. It's time you were invited to new arenas of your sport. It starts now. Behemoth.

5

SCHEDULED TIME OFF, BUT NOT FOR VACATION

One of the greatest things about your job is scheduled time off. You know what I'm talking about – all plans are complete and the waiting game has begun. You've got vacation time waiting for you and you can see the light at the end of the tunnel. You've schedule time away from the office, and you can't wait. Inevitably, what happens when you get back from your time off? You feel refreshed, rejuvenated, ready to conquer the mountain of tasks that piled up while you were gone. Trust me – this will not be what you experience in this program.

The last thing you'll want to do is hit an off week with this program. You're going to see gains like you've never realized and lifting will be one of the most fun things in your life. You'll love it. You'll crave time spent with the bar in your grasp. And, I know what you'll do – you'll try to push it. You'll feel good and think you can push your training a few weeks without taking time off. I know what it's like. I have been, and am, there with you, my friend.

I will tell you, though, I've pushed it and skipped off weeks, but I always pay for it. I hit plateaus and over train, simply because I love lifting so much. I've been injured, forcing me to spend weeks or months out of training completely, all because I ignored my body and the protocols I had put in place.

In college I didn't understand this whatsoever. I used to train four days a week, two and a half hours lifting each day. I'd finish my workout and then do more stuff. One year I even did two-a-days for much of the year – I didn't feel like my coach's workout was hard enough, so I'd do my own workout, do his, then throw for two hours or more, and finish up with conditioning. I was one amazing example of over training. I couldn't understand why I wasn't seeing improvement on a consistent basis. I was training up to five hours a day between lifting, throwing and conditioning. Throw in a full load of classes, multiple campus ministries, track meets, varsity athlete club, and ministries at my local church and I don't know how I survived. Oh, and the last two years I was wooing my now wife, which was a full-time job alone! Only by the grace of God did I not wind up with serious injuries during my track career (I had some substantial wrist pain and broke my own finger, but nothing serious). I didn't understand why other guys took time off. I just figured I wanted it more, which I did, but I paid for it. When I'd have consecutive days, or weeks, of being run down and having really weak lifts I just chalked it up as an off day or two and told myself that was when I made myself a man – that training hard through those days would pay huge dividends in the future. Boy, was I wrong. Don't do this! Learn from my stupidity!

The only weeks off I took were the weeks of the conference and National Championship track meets. Ironically, I had my best throws at the conference meet each year! Bingo, McKim, you're fresh! Enjoy a big throw or two! Now, in the next chapter we'll go over timing and programming for you to peak at your optimal meets or games, but you would have thought something would have clicked with me, seeing my big throws come like that.

I look back now and want to punch myself in the face for not being smarter. I sometimes wonder what I could have thrown had I done what I know now. I might have thrown the shot put longer and never picked up the Highland Games. Who knows? I also almost played baseball my freshmen year of high school instead of throwing shot put and discus. Had I done that, I am sure of a few things: I would have struck out a lot, been hit by a multitude of pitches, not played infield (scared of the ball) and probably rode the bench. Its memories like these when I thank God for where He's taken me and what He's done with me. God is so good.

So, you'll try to push it. You'll probably even skip an off week, thinking I don't know what I'm talking about. While I don't know much, I know my experiences, and know them well – the off week is a critical piece of programming. Keep the off week. It'll make you so stinkin' hungry to get back in you'll tear it up in the next cycle. Get in the gym and hit two very light days of training (preferably split it into an upper day and lower day). Then, come time for the next phase, you'll be a determined behemoth with that iron. Again, it will be hard to take the week off, but it's imperative that you do. Here are a few things that I do, and have done, to distract me and keep my sanity during my off week.

1. Go in for one or two days and just do some light your work. Keep it low key, as I prefer you not even go in, but I understand how important routine can be to overall health and recovery in a strength program.

2. Hit up some basketball or racquetball or something you don't normally do. Challenge a buddy to some 1 on 1, clay pigeons or skee ball. I don't care what it is, just do something. Get competitive without tearing yourself down.

3. Go for walks.

4. Find the stress release in something besides lifting -- video games, catch up on a movie you've wanted to see, watch a few hours of videos on YouTube for technical training of your sport, etc.

I know it's hard and frustrating, but with you hitting it hard for five days, your body needs that week to recover, or else you'll wind up in a place you don't like – the injured reserve.

6

PROGRAMMING FOR PEAK PERFORMANCE

If you're doing this program in the off-season, don't worry about peaking. All I want you to worry about is getting to the gym and doing this workout. You'll grow. You'll develop. You'll be a behemoth. Eat. It. Up.

For me, in the Highland Games, there are really two games I want to peak for each year: US and World Championships. The US Championship is always the last weekend in September, while the World Championship will rotate on a yearly basis, both in site and date. This can make programming difficult, especially if they are multiple weeks apart.

I recommend you find a meet, game, games, or match that you want to be the strongest for. Ideally, you'd want to set the end of the full Behemoth program to coincide with your event. Every athlete is different, but I've found that I have about two weeks of "peak" competitive sports performance where I've backed off my training. I can sometimes stretch that to three weeks, but if you're closing in on conference or Nationals, the playoffs, state finals, or the end of your season, and you must back off to stay healthy and recovered, you'll have about two to three weeks of optimal, fresh strength. The key is, don't let it get longer than that if you want to stay on top of your strength performance. The greatest advice I can give you for doing this program in season is twofold:

    1. Come to grips that you'll be training through the first bit of your season with the realization you'll be that much stronger and more athletic at the end, when it really matters. This is where you'll have to fight your ego, as you'll want to be 100% awesome 100% of the time. This, sadly, is not possible. For the throwers, throw bombs when it really counts, on the biggest stage of the year. If you don't believe me, look at all the top throwing programs and see when they have their biggest throws each season. For my fellow Scottish athletes, look at distances set at the biggest stages like Pleasanton, the Celtic Classic, Halkirk, and others. These are all late in the season, set by the best athletes in the sport. Whether you're a novice, master or Pro, your class's best marks are set at games like these. There is a reason for this, and I believe building your program to peak at the right time is critical.

I've done the hard work for you with Behemoth.

    2. Not only is this set for you to peak at the end of it, but there are multiple small peak "windows" built into it. Every four weeks your body is given a chance to reset and recover for the phase ahead. These allow for you to establish peak time periods within your season and within your programming. I believe these are critical for Scottish Highland Games athletes and track and field throwers. While you'll want to ultimately peak for the end of the season, you'll need a few weeks of peak throwing strength and focus along the way, whether that's to get your qualifying mark in to an athletic director of a games, build name recognition, get a qualifying mark for Nationals or move up the pecking order of your team. Behemoth takes the guess work out for you. It's set to peak for huge throws at the end of the year, while allowing you to

experience small windows of recovery during the meat of your season.

The important thing to remember is that you must have something you are training for. You must have an end goal that all this is building towards. This program can be a grind. To me, it's fun and you'll be ecstatic with the growth, but when you're near the point of vomiting during squats or feel buried by the mental struggle that can come from cleans and snatches, you've got to dig deep and remember what you're striving for. Think about how sweet it will be to celebrate with your team. Picture yourself on the podium. Imagine them calling for the steel tape to measure your record throw. These are the things that keep you going. These are the experiences you are working towards. You'll enjoy them later, because of the work you put in now.

7

THREE PHASES: SINEWS, BRONZE, IRON

Behemoth is broken into three phases of the program: Sinews, Bronze, Iron. You'll notice that I've named these along the scripture verse that describes Behemoth. Read that passage again and you'll see why I named the below as such – if we're going to build you into a monster, we need to know how to do it! By changing phases after four weeks each, you're challenging and pushing your body to adapt to the new stressors.

<u>SINEWS</u>
This first phase is summed up as the, "high rep," or, "volume," phase, to put it simply. It encompasses sets of 12 or 10. Higher reps like this help your body get the volume in it needs to foster growth and development. Right off the bat, you'll notice that your clothes are fitting different as you push it to new levels with the rep count. If you're like me, you spent years figuring submaximal lifts at this count were detrimental to your development as a strength athlete. If we are to build the power and strength your body needs to compete at the top of your game, then we must build a strong foundation with volume. You will be sore and squat days will be miserable. You're building for the next phases. Trust me, you'll enjoy the next two phases much better.

<u>BRONZE</u>
Sets in the middle range characterize this phase. Now that you've build a solid foundation with volume work, your body is ready to add more weight to the training regimen. You're still not "maxing," nor are you finding yourself buried with percentages you can't reach. Push yourself. Do as much weight as you can for each set. What I find interesting about this phase, though, is that you very well may begin lifting your prior maxes as your working sets by week eight or nine of Behemoth. It's times like this where the excitement level is so high you just want to train all the time. The hunger is setting in and you're becoming Behemoth. This phase will also usher in some changes to your accessory lifts and cleans and snatches. The idea with these changes is to keep things fresh to avoid burnout and to challenge your body as it is starting to adapt to the programming. Confusing and challenging your body to perform new exercises will pay dividends as you go.

<u>IRON</u>
Now that you've built a solid foundation with volume work and ushered in a more powerful you, it's time to finish it with the strength phase. The first few weeks of the Strength phase you are, again, challenging your body with more weight and lower rep counts. Load it up. Push your body to its limits with as much weight as you can handle. This is a great phase as you're prepping to max, which is the reward for all the hard work you've done. I believe in about one week, maybe two, of true one-rep max work. Your body finds it hard to recover from things such as this, so let's keep it to a minimum and celebrate. You'll love this phase. Not only are

you prepping for the peak we talked about earlier, but you're about to see how much you've truly grown on Behemoth. Strength training has few times as great as this.

8

THE BEHEMOTH DIET & SUPPLEMENTS

I'm not a dietician, physician or medical professional. As always, with any training program, consult your doctor. While I do believe supplements are helpful in the growth and development of an athlete who is training hard, I don't get too complicated with what I take or recommend:

Behemoth Diet
Eat. Eat often and eat a lot. Better yet, make it meat with a side of meat. Again, Behemoth is not for every athlete, but for athletes looking to be more powerful. To do this, you'll need fuel. Feed yourself so you can recover from the training you're doing. Here's a very simple skeleton version of a meal plan, structured for those of us fitting the Behemoth mold.
This is simply a guide that I use and is for you to build from – for more in depth help or specific needs, talk with a dietician. If you do, I might suggest someone of size who understands your needs on a more personal level.

Breakfast
Coffee
½ cup oatmeal or grits
2-6 eggs

Post-workout
1-2 scoops protein
1 scoop wazy maize starch or 1 tablespoon honey
1 teaspoon creatine
(mix together with water or other liquid of choice)

Mid-morning
8+ oz. meat (steak, burger, chicken, pork, fish, turkey, venison)
Cup of rice, fruit, baked potato, pasta, nuts, etc.

Lunch
Full meal of your choice—leftovers from the night before work great on the diet and the budget

Mid-afternoon
2 scoops protein
1 teaspoon creatine
-or-
Repeat Mid-Morning snack

Dinner
Full meal of your choice. Meat must be on the menu each night, as you're going to need all that you can handle.

Night Snack
PB&J
Glass of milk
-or- Protein shake, eggs, etc.

Creatine
Creatine is great to aid in recovery and muscle growth. As always, you should be downing one to two gallons of water a day, anyways, but because it works to push water into your muscles, give it plenty to work with. I keep it simple and take a dose right after I lift and then another dose later on that day.

Fish Oil
Fish Oil helps with your joints and soreness. Honestly, every athlete should be taking this, but especially athletes who are larger and may be putting more stress on their bodies.

Branch Chain Amino Acids (BCAAs)
BCAAs are great for recovery and energy. I highly recommend you make a practice of consuming these during your competition as well. For my fellow highland games athletes, pack these for your long day. You should be sipping on these throughout the day. Most any, "intraworkout" supplement is a good option, here.

Waxy Maize Starch
This is another critical supplement for your intra-event competing. For those long days and competitions, you'll need carbs and calories, and Waxy Maize Starch is an amazing way to get it instantly. I like to drink starch and creatine right after my workout with a protein shake.

Protein Powder
I like to stick with isolate protein over concentrate, as my body seems to react much better to the isolate, and break it down better. Aim for a minimum of 25 grams of protein after your workout with 50 grams being best.

Pre-workout
If you want something to help you get energized and ready for your training session, a pre-workout may help you. I'm not a big fan of all the stimulants many of the companies put into their mix, but a large number of athletes find these helpful. I've tried various pre-workout blends, but the best I've found yet is coffee. Yep, coffee. Explore what's best for you, but be careful to read your labels and don't take something that's banned. You alone are responsible for that.

But, aside from all this, seeing gains is pretty simple in that, if you give me 100% effort on this program and eat a healthy dose of food, you'll grow. This concept was exampled to me fairly simply in a lunch meeting with a Strength and Conditioning Coach from a Division I school in the Midwest. We were discussing how to train and program for collegiate athletes. In a time when everyone wants to break down everything from food to percentages, we discussed what truly matters. I think it applies to you whether you're being coached, are on our own, are an adult training yourself, strength athlete, or only reading this because it was gifted to you:

He said, "You talk to coaches and know your stuff. To you, what makes the best strength coaches out there?"

Wow. How's that for being put on the spot?
I leaned back into my chair (rest assured, it did not break … creaked somethin' fierce, but didn't break), and ate another chip dunked liberally in salsa. My response was pretty simple, but challenging for me, and him, I think. Let me explain.

I told him that, in all honesty, it's not hard to make an 18-22 year old strong. As long as they eat and spend time under the bar, they're going to get strong and fast. Any coach can do that. Any coach can build a program. Any coach can hand out a sheet of exercises. Any coach can copy and paste some strong guy's workout from the internet – complete with percentages, periodization, undulating pyramids, hypertrophy out the ears and phases for any time of the year!

It was at this point in the lunch I was afraid I offended him, but I had already eaten my main course, so I wasn't as concerned with leaving the restaurant early. He smirked out the side of his mouth and agreed with me. He said, "You're right, this isn't hard."

Great. Smooth move, McKim. There goes a potential customer!
"There's more to it, isn't there?" He folded his arms.

I went on to explain further. I told him how the first thing I noticed about the weight room he managed was the environment, culture and "vibe" (that last word is for all you 80's children). I told him how I could easily tell he was building, and had built, something greater than just a place for athletes to move weights. I told him that, in my opinion, the best coaches are the ones who relate to the athletes and can motivate them. The best coaches can foster growth beyond the weight room. The best coaches do more than just spit out workouts and unlock the doors in the morning. The best coaches know their athletes outside of the weight room or athletic field. The best coaches invest. The best coaches care. The best coaches love.

While we were discussing the relationship between the athlete and a good strength coach, I think the same goes for you. Anyone can follow a program. Anyone can grab onto a workout and give it a shot. But, to really be successful, you've got to want it. You've got to care. You've got to love it. Is training a, "job"for you? If so, then you probably won't last long in it. It's not always going to be fun and you won't always experience huge gains. But, if you'll enjoy the journey do more than just follow this workout, you won't be disappointed where you'll end up. In all honesty, you won't want to leave it.

9

TECHNIQUE, TRAINING GEAR AND GENERAL POINTS OF CONTENTION

Lifting Straps
A number of athletes and coaches feel straps are a hindrance to your cleans and snatches. Aside from limiting your wrist flexibility (helpful in "catching" or "racking" the clean), straps do not keep you from developing areas you'll need in athletic performance. It all actuality, I believe they help you. Olympic movements from the hang position are especially hard on grip strength, which will limit the amount of weight you can do. Don't let your grip limit the development of your other parts of the body. I recommend you strap up. Unless you're a competitive Olympic lifter, there's no reason not to use straps. If you're a football player, use other avenues to develop your grip strength (grippers, towel pull ups, rice bucket, fat grip pull downs, etc.).

Knee Wraps
I wear a light knee sleeve to keep my knees warm (blue Rehbands work great), but I'm not a fan of tight knee wraps, personally. I used them pretty heavily for a number of months but starting getting a good deal of knee pain. Some may say I'm being a hypocrite by using lifting straps by not knee wraps, but I can only state my preference. If you do choose to use wraps, please realize they are helping you a minimum of 5-10% in the squats. I also believe the hinder the strength and development of your stabilizing muscles around the knee. If you choose to use them, please limit the use to sets in the Iron Phase.

Bench Shirts, Briefs, Suits
Same goes for these types of equipment. These are for powerlifters, which I am not and, most likely, neither are you. We're training to be stronger on the field not exactly to be stronger with equipment like this. Unless you're a powerlifter, you shouldn't be training with these.

Belt
I use a belt for my hang cleans and snatches as well as squats. I do, however, limit my use of it for the last one or two sets when my body is more tired and technique wavering (and the weight is heavier).

Bench Press Technique
There are a number of throwers and athletes who believe a "dynamic bench" is best for shot putters and even linemen. For years I was one in this camp, but for the sole reason that it made me bench more. I hate saying it, but I think we all can, honestly, agree with that. A "dynamic bench" is where you arch the back high and even bounce the bar off your chest. Feel free to hit my YouTube page and you'll see a number of my bench videos. See what I mean? Conversely, in 2013, I began doing stricter bench pressing and enjoyed it greatly. I've since gone away from a "dynamic bench" and now keep my butt on the bench and just touch the bar to my chest. No heaving. No bouncing. I made this change in preparation for the 2014 Arnold Classic Championship and saw great results. Due to the weather in Missouri during the late winter, my

training was very limited in preparation for this big event. Yet, after only touching a stone a few times in five months, I blasted a new personal best in the open stone. I can't say that stricter bench pressing was the sole reason for improvement, but I felt stronger and believe it was to my benefit.

Squat Depth
One of the things I hate seeing in the gym is lousy squats. Squats well above parallel pain me not only for the lack of muscular development, but in the false sense of strength they give you. I am a firm believer in the bar being in a high position on your back, feet about shoulder width apart (or closer), toes pointed in a more neutral stance, and the depth deep. Deep as in your butt should touch your calves. Since I've been squatting this way (a couple of years now), my knees have thanked me. When you drop below parallel, the stress is moved from your knees to your hips, which is a much larger joint. For the first few weeks, your hips will be very sore and you'll question your technique altering. Stick with it. The power and strength you are developing will help you in your lifts and onthe field.

I'll never forget one morning in the gym when I was getting some squats in. A few guys were watching in awe of me, but it wasn't because of the weight, as it's no secret I am not a gifted squatter. I do not have large or sizeable legs. In high school I was called, "Johnny Bravo," due to my disproportionally larger upper body, chicken legs, big hair … and lack of decent pick-up lines for the ladies.

"How do you do that?" this guy said as I racked the bar. I looked at the weight and realized quickly he wasn't talking about the number of 45s on the bar. "What do you mean?" I asked. "You get so low. I'm going to get there eventually; I'm still working on hip flexibility."

I watched this man do quarter squats in the rack next to me wondering what he meant by, "working on hip flexibility." It is pretty clear to me, but it's comes down to something that many athletes struggle with – ego. Lighten the weight and drop your butt into the hole. Your body's movement shouldn't be to stop from going down, but to explode out of the hole of the squat. Drive the heels into the ground like you're trying to push holes into the floor. Don't let the knees wobble in and out as you stand up. If you're not willing to humble yourself, then you're not willing to give what it takes to be a Behemoth.

10

A WORD FROM YOUR LOCAL D.A.R.E. ROLE MODEL

Stay away from drugs. It's as simple as that. Sadly, drugs have grown into a very prominent place in strength sports and it doesn't look like that will change anytime soon. I would like to encourage each and every one of you to avoid the myriad of drugs that will be, or already are, readily available to you. Steroids to HGH, a growing number of athletes are even seeing prescriptions from a doctor to tell them that they should get injected with testosterone. In the years past, this was called "steroids," and "cheating." Today, people are calling it a remedy. Please don't understand this as a write off of all hormone treatment, as there are people in society who need medication to help with the changes they are facing. Nine times out of 10, though, these people are not athletes. These people aren't looking to improve substantially in a sport, win more money in competition, take places on the podium, be on the first team, win their pro card, etc. Yes, this workout is tough. Yes, you'll be really sore, but, this isn't a time to turn to artificial help to aid in you getting bigger and more explosive in half the time. Work hard! You can handle it and you'll enjoy the gains coming your way, but again, you owe it to yourself, your family, your future family, your friends, your teammates, your athletic directors and coaches, and your competitors to remain clean. The future, and present, ramifications of taking performance enhancing drugs can change your life.

Please know that I am a lifetime drug-free athlete – I have made this commitment to God, my family and my former, current and future competitors. Behemoth is tough, but certainly in the realm for a clean athlete to not only perform all the workouts, but to thrive while doing it. If you, too, are a clean athlete, you'll enjoy Behemoth and know that it was built and field-tested by a lifetime clean athlete.

11
EXERCISE DESCRIPTIONS

ABS/CORE

AB WHEEL: Using an actual ab wheel or makeshift version from round plates on your barbell, kneel down and roll out until your face almost touches the ground. Return to the original position. For variances in this, try rolling out with an arch to the right side, then left, then center; roll out, hold your position just above the ground, and "punch" your arms straight out in from of you as many times as possible before falling. I sometimes like to roll out and even hold my position for a five second count. Sorinex makes what is called the, "Gluteham Roller," which is great for this exercise, in addition to the lower extremity movements.

PLANKS: Hold your body up on your elbows and toes. Hold this position. Target a 30 second or more hold. For variances, try side planks, planks while rolling your hips from side to side, etc.

CRUNCHES: fold hands over chest, crunch up to bent knees.

LEG LIFTS: Hold onto bench head while feet are off the ground, straight. Slide down so your butt is at the end of the bench. Lift legs up and down. For a challenge, left legs up, then shoot them straight into the air towards the ceiling while coming back down slowly.

WINDSHIELD WIPERS: Laying on floor, hold onto a rack, stationary bar, etc. and hold your legs just inches off the ground. Sway your feet back and forth, all the way up even with your shoulder level.

MEDBALL SIT UP: Hold a medicine ball over your head while your feet are on the ground in a sit up position. As you sit up, overhead throw the ball to a partner or against the wall. Catch, and return slowly to the start position.

GLUTEHAM SIT UPS: Flip over on the gluteham and do sit ups from there, at the level or depth that you can safely do.

GLUTEHAM/BACK HYPER TWISTS: Lay, as normal, in the gluteham developer or back hyper, and hold a med ball or plate out in front of you, face towards the ground. Twist side to side while holding the plate or ball straight out in front of you.

PLATE TWISTS: Stand with your feet shoulder width apart, knees slightly bent. Hold a weight plate out in front of you, twisting side to side. Mentally focus on bracing your mid-section by pulling your belly button into your back.

SIDE TO SIDE PLATE/BAL: Sit on your butt. Cross your feet with your knees bent and close to your chest. With both hands, grip a weight plate or medicine ball on one side of your body. While holding your feet off the ground, move the ball or plate side to side without touching your body.

SIDE THROWS: Grab a medicine ball with both hands while standing perpendicular to a wall. Rotate your body and throw the ball into the wall. Catch, return to the original position and throw again. Do this without stopping until rep count complete. Switch sides.

CHEST

BENCH PRESS: Lie down on the bench with your feet firmly planted on the ground. Place your hands on the bar with your thumbs wrapped around it (please, do not fold your thumbs behind the bar – too many people lose the bar and wind up getting hurt). Place your hands at a comfortable width, but greater than shoulder width is recommended. Do not bounce or "heave" the bar off your chest. Butt is to remain on the bench.

CLOSE GRIP BENCH: Set up just like the bench press, only place your hands in a much closer position. Hand position should be set up with your pinkies in-line with your armpit line. Again, no bouncing or "heaving" the bar off your chest.

INCLINE PRESS: Lie down on a bench set at a 45 degree angle. With your feet firmly planted on the ground, place your hands on the bar at a spot just slightly more narrow than your grip for the bench press. Lower the bar to just below your chin so it touches your chest. Press the bar back up, fully extending the arms.

DIPS: With your arms fully extended and legs crossed and bent up towards you to allow clearance off the ground. Lower your body down by bending your arms. When your chest is level with your hands, press your body back to the start position. Weights can be suspended between the legs or bands placed across the shoulders for increased resistance.

PUSHUPS: Lie on the floor with your palms on the ground, placed as wide as your armpits. With your legs straight, press your body up. Focus on keeping the body straight and completing full reps. No short or "pulsing" movements in this exercise. Raise and lower your body the whole way. A weight vest, partner forced resistance reps, weight, or bands across the shoulders all add additional resistance should it be needed.

FLYS: These can be performed via a peck deck machine, dumbbells, weight stacks, etc. However you're doing them, concentrate on "squeezing" the chest. If these are done with dumbbells, please, don't go crazy on it. This is more of a mobility and "health" exercise as I want you to get the blood flowing. More than "feeling the stretch" I'd rather you hold it at the top.

PULLLOVER AND PRESS: Lie on your back on a bench. Using a curl bar, hold it at your chest with your hands roughly shoulder-width apart, perhaps closer. With your elbows in tight, lower the bar just over your head and face until it almost touches the ground behind your head. Pull the bar back over your head into the starting position. Once reached, press the bar away from you like a close grip bench press. Return the bar to the staring position and perform the allotted number of reps. For a challenge upon completion of the reps, rapidly press the bar out until failure.

TRICEPS

CABLE EXTENSION: Keep the elbows in close to your body and simply extend the arms. As the weeks go on, change up the bar you use for variety.

OVERHEAD ROPE EXTENSION: At your cable machine/stack, use the rope attachment and turn your back to the stack. Use either one hand or two, change it up, and extend your hands, completely, over your head.

BANDED TRICEP EXTENSION: Use a band to do various triceps work to improve blood flow, recovery and strength. Work in various exercises like overhead extension, "kick backs" (keep the arm in tight to your side, lean over parallel to the ground and extend the arm completely.

OVERHEAD DUMBBELL EXTENSION: Much like the overhead rope extension exercise, use a dumbbell, holding one at a time. Try to lower the dumbbell to the opposite shoulder than the arm you are using. This should be done behind the head.

SKULL CRUSHERS: lie flat on a bench with your elbows in tight and your palms by your forehead, facing out away from you (thus, the name, "skull crushers"). Extend your arms up away from your face.

ANY MACHINE OR VARIATION YOU CAN THINK OF: Be creative. Do any triceps work that you can think of. Don't over think this and don't get too regimented. Try something new or even do some machines – they aren't all bad.

CLEANS/SNATCHES

RACK CLEAN: Set your bar and loaded weights onto a raised apparatus. This can be boxes, a rack's safety bars, "scoops" from a rack, plyo/step up boxes, etc. Set this height where the bar is just above your kneecap. The whole point of this exercise is to load your body to the bar and clean it up without any downward or upward movement at the start. This is a flat-out explosion lift. Your hands should be placed, roughly, a thumb's width from the inside of the bar knurling. Concentrate on a big shrug with your shoulders, followed by extending the hips. As the bar travels up towards your chin, quickly move your elbows under the bar and "shoot" them forward. You should "catch" the bar (the finishing position) on your collar bone or, if your flexibility allows, up close to your throat like you are about to perform a front squat. You should "catch" the bar in a semi-squat power position. Do not over-extend yourself, but your legs will, and should, splay out a bit (in other words, do not over-extend yourself, but understand your legs will shoot out some). Do not concentrate on pulling your clean just high enough for you to do a full front squat – front squats are on Fridays. You must focus on a big pull, full extension and fast elbows. Stand up with the bar still in the "catch" position. Reset the bar onto the apparatus and perform the next rep.

HANG CLEAN: Perform this lift just as described for the "Rack Clean," only start with the bar in the "hang" position. Hold the bar with your arms relaxed (the bar should hang at about mid-quad height). To start the lift, you'll have a natural lean forward, which will drop the bar right close to your kneecaps.

RACK SNATCH: Set your bar and loaded weights onto a raised apparatus. The load should rest on the plates or bumpers which will allow you to have your hands at the appropriate snatch grip site. This hand placement will differ for each person based on comfort, height and arm length. I'm 6'5" with an average wingspan, but I have my hands placed all the way out to where the bar sleeve begins. If you watch Olympic weightlifters, most all of them place their hands here, regardless of height. It truly is a comfort thing, but close grip snatches should only be done for a change of pace. The apparatus you place the load on can be boxes, a rack's technique scoops, plyo/step up boxes, etc. – anything that will allow you clearance for your hands to be placed on the bar. Set this height where the bar is at lower-mid quad height. The whole point of this exercise is to load your body to the bar and snatch it up without any downward or upward movement at the start. This is a flat-out explosion lift. Concentrate on a big shrug with your shoulders, followed by extending the hips. As the bar travels up towards your chin, quickly move your head forward, or "shoot" it through the hole your arms are now making. If you mentally think of "shooting" your head through that hole when the bar is at your chin, you'll make it there at the right time. Too many times people forget this step, but it is the most critical to you finishing the lift – the head must make it through that window quickly. You should "catch" the bar, overhead, in a semi-squat power position. Do not splay your legs out wide, but your legs will, and should, splay out a bit (in other words, do not over-extend yourself, but understand your legs will shoot out some). Do not concentrate on pulling your snatch just high enough for you to do a full overhead squat. Remember, we're training to make you a better athlete, not an Olympic lifter – you don't need to do full squat snatches for this athletic advancement. You must focus on a big pull, full extension and a fast head through the window/hole. Stand up with the bar still in the "catch" position. Reset the bar onto the apparatus and perform the next rep.

HANG SNATCH: Perform this lift just as described for the "Rack Snatch," only start with the bar in the "hang" position. Hold the bar with your arms relaxed (the bar should hang at about mid-quad height). To start the lift, you'll have a natural lean forward, which will drop the bar right close to your kneecaps. Pull and complete the lift.

LEGS

BACK SQUAT: It is my experience that a high bar, "Olympic" version of the back squat relates best to athletic performance. Again, this is my opinion and experience in my sport. I am not overtly against low-bar position squats, I just don't feel they translate as well. For this program, you will be doing high-bar, closer stance, deep squats. By "high bar," I mean that the bar will set at the top of your traps and upper back. Some people find this uncomfortable and will try to use a pad, wrapped towel or bracing attachment to relieve some of the discomfort. Don't. Don't do this. Your goal is to squat heavier and deeper than you ever have, and any sort of additional measures like this will only hinder you in the long run. It will take roughly three weeks for your body to adjust to the new bar position and you'll be glad for it soon. The placement of your hands on the bar is up to your personal preference. I like to get my hands fairly close as it helps keep my back tight and chest out. Some lifters prefer a very wide grip, but that seems to be mostly due to upper body flexibility. Find your comfortable groove, but make it consistent and try to get them in closer. Your feet should be shoulder width apart with your toes pointed forward with a slight turn to the outside (not straight ahead forward, not pigeon-toed, but not pointed out sideways, either). After you un-rack the bar and walk it out into the rack, take a big, deep breath before you even begin your descent. Brace your mid-section with that breath and descend to the bottom of your squat. Don't make it a slow descent, either – you're only wasting your energy by slowly dropping into the bottom. In terms of depth, we covered that in an earlier chapter, but there's no need for your training partner to "check depth" or for you to video your squats just to make sure you hit parallel. You will not hit parallel – you'll cruise on past it. You'll know you've gone deep enough when you hit the bottom ... as in your bottom to your calves. Your depth for both back and front squats should be at this level. Save your knees, check your ego and get better at your sport.

LUNGES: I am not a fan of stationary lunges (just lunging in place). I prefer a barbell on the back or weights in your hands. Lunge long and hard – your knee should just "kiss" the ground. DO NOT SLAM your knee to the ground; rather, just brush it as you lunge.

DIAMOND BAR JUMPS: Step into the middle of a loaded diamond or "trap" bar. Grab the handles and explode from the floor into a full jump. Try to keep the bar in a neutral or stationary position during "flight." In other words, don't pull the bar up by bending your elbows or performing an exaggerated shrug with the bar. Doing this will more complicate your landing, not only increasing your likelihood of injury, but throwing your rhythm off for multiple jumps. Land softly on the balls of your feet, recoiling into the next jump – the bar should return to the floor, but do not slam or bounce it for your next jump. Do not land with your knees locked. Focus on jumping through the roof – do not allow yourself to be comfortable with simply hopping with weight in your hands.

GLUTEHAM/BACK HYPER: I prefer you use a Gluteham Developer over a 45 degree back hyper, but do what you can with what you have. As you develop and grow, hold a plate or dumbbell at your chest, or add a band around your back and the legs of the Gluteham for added resistance. Concentrate on squeezing your glutes towards the top and stretching your hamstrings at the bottom. For a "poor man's" version of the Gluteham, have someone hold your feet down while you're on your knees. Slowly lower your chest to the ground. Go back to the starting position and do it again.

STRAIGHT LEG DEADS: Just when you thought I didn't have any deads in my program, I have one, and it's not really a dead lift. I will do these with a cable machine or bands, but not a barbell or dumbbells. The key in this lift, for the Highland Games, is to raise the arms with you as you extend. You're working on strength, but it's also a closely-related lift to the weight over bar event. This simple exercise corresponds to many sports in the BEHEMOTH scheme of things, but relates best to Scottish Highland Games (what do you expect, it's what I do!). For banded straight leg deads, wrap a band around a solid structure. The band strength should be large on this, as you'll be working a large muscle group. Walk out a bit from the structure, straddling the band. Keep your legs straight, grab the band, and accelerate your hands out in front of you. Keep the arms straight. This should be fast and explosive. Fire your posterior to accelerate the hands. Reach back, fire the posterior.

ROMANIAN DEADLIFTS: This deadlift is also for accessory work and shouldn't be considered a "core" exercise to the program. Lift the bar off the rack like you would for hang cleans. Bending the knees and leaning over, lower the bar down your legs until you reach the top of your kneecaps or slightly lower, depending on your wing span (longer armed athletes will need to lower the bar further for full effectiveness). As you bring the bar back up to the start position, rotate the hips forward, squeezing your glutes hard and extending the hips. This is the focus for this lift – glute activation and hip extension. THIS IS NOT A BACK EXERCISE OR A GOOD MORNING. HIPS! GLUTES!

LEG CURLS: This is the standard leg curl machine that is in every fitness center and commercial gym. Switch it up between double-leg and single-leg work. You also do this exercise by lying on your back and placing your heels on furniture sliders. Slide the feet up and down to work the hamstrings and glutes. Some people also use towels on a wood floor to perform this exercise, while I prefer the Sorinex Gluteham Roller.

HIP THRUSTERS: Lie flat on your back. Move your feet toward your butt, placing them flat-footed on the ground a foot or so away from your butt. Thrust your hips into the air, squeezing the glutes at the top. Place a bar across your lap for added resistance. As you get comfortable with these, add resistance in the form of a bar or bands.

BACKWARDS HILL/STAIRCASE CLIMB: Whether on a hill or up steps, turn around and go up them backwards. Hold weight in your hands or a barbell on your back. Focus on pushing your way up the incline, as you'll feel it in the quads. This is a great exercise for quad health and patella tendonitis. Increase weight or distance as you get better. I would start with a few flights of stairs as one set, moving up from there.

BANDED/CABLE KNEE EXTENSION: Wrap a band around a solid structure and step your leg into the loop. The band should rest on the backside of your knee. Move back until you have a solid pull against your leg. Start with a bent knee and foot up on your toes. Extend your leg and push your heel to the ground. Hold briefly in the extended position. This exercise can also be performed by using a cable column instead of a band.

STEP UPS: These should be done with a barbell on your back, stepping onto a plyo box or bench. One rep per leg equals one total rep. Keep the bar high on your back and step back down carefully and with strength from your other leg. DO NOT SLAM back to the floor.

FRONT SQUATS: If you lack the flexibility to "rack" the bar across your shoulders and collarbone, place lifting straps tight around the bar. Place the bar deep into your neck and shoulders and grab the long straps with your hands. Pretend they are an extension of you, allowing you to "rack" the bar properly, while controlling the bar. A key to remember in this lift is to place that bar in as deep against your throat as possible. You're gonna feel like you might pass out, and you might even start to blackout the first time you try it, but you'll get a groove. Doing this lines up your squat so much better. Should you start to lose it, don't fight it and risk injury. Let the bar fall in front and push it away from you.

BACK

LAT PULLS: Do these on the standard lat pull machine. Hand placement should be wide, and the finish position of the lift should be in front, pulling the bar to your collar bone. Do not pull down behind your neck. If you don't have a machine, used bands attached to a rack and brace yourself on the ground or a bench to accommodate the resistance. Ideally, a lat pull machines is best, but improvise and work with what you have access to.

PULL UPS: I understand pull ups are hard for Behemoths, but they are very important. Don't worry; you'll get better at them. If you need help, use a large band to assist you, if needed, or a training partner. Wrap the long band around the bar, with the loop at your feet. Place your feet in the loop and start doing pull ups. The band will assist you on the way up. I like to change up my pull ups. Here's a few for you to consider:
- Hands facing each other (parallel grip pull ups)
- Wide, lat pull grip pull
- Towel: place a towel over the bar and grip each ends with your hands. This is also great for grip development
- Fatbar/fat grip pull ups
- Reverse grip pull ups
- Weight pull ups
- Rack pull ups (instead of a bar, use the blocky structure of your rack)
- Hand grenade/rack balls/baseball/pool ball pull ups. Attach these to your structure with straps, chains, etc.
- Ring pull ups
- Rope pull ups (perform these like towel pull ups, or let your imagination go wild)
- If you have a rock wall, do some pull ups there
- Steel beam/flat surface pull ups

SEATED ROWS: This lift is performed on a cable machine you'll find at most facilities. Change up your grip by using various handle attachments as well as rope, towels, balls, etc. Concentrate on squeezing your shoulder blades. To me, there are two critical aspects of lat/back development. Lats – pull ups, lat pulls, anything pulling down from overhead. Rhomboids – rows, dumbbell rows, inverted pullups, anything pulling toward you at a neutral or low height.

INVERTED ROWS: In a rack or similar apparatus, lay on the ground with a barbell in place just past arms' length. With your legs straight, pull yourself up to the bar, touching your chest if possible. As you get tired, or until you're able to do this lift fully, bring your feet closer to you to help relieve some of the weight. As you advance in this exercise, place weight or arrange bands across your mid-section to add resistance.

CHEST SUPPORTED ROWS: Whether it's dumbbells with your body flipped backwards on an incline bench or "T" bar rows with your body overhanging a bench, this exercise is exactly as it states. Again, make sure you are squeezing the shoulder blades together for each rep. Pull the bar to your chest or the dumbbell to your arm pit.

BICEPS

BAR CURLS: Stand while holding the bar with a supinated grip. Grip width should be just outside your legs while holding the bar in the down position. Keep the elbows in and pull the bar up to your chin. Return to the start position in a controlled manner. For this exercise, change it up – use a straight 45 pound bar, an actual curl bar, reverse grip for more forearm work, wide grip, seated, standing, seated on an incline bench, etc.

DUMBBELL HAMMER CURLS: Hold dumbbells at your side with a grip like you would use to drive nails with (thus, the name "hammer," as you are moving the dumbbells up and down like a hammer). You can alternate one arm at a time, but curling each arm simultaneously is more difficult.

DUMBBELL CURLS: Standard dumbbell curl – seated with elbow braced on your thigh like you see in every commercial or show where someone is working out. Try this standing up, chest supported, arms out and parallel with the floor, etc. Be creative.

ROPE/TOWEL CURLS: Use a cable stack/low lat pull station and place the rope attachment on it or a towel. Grip this and begin curling with it.

Any other bicep exercise you can dream up or see in the gym. This day is meant for accessory work and strengthening the back , biceps and forearms. These muscle groups, while not a primary focus, provide a great amount of assist and functional help in other lifts and sport specific events.

SHOULDERS

INCLINE PRESS: Much like the bench press, this exercise is done against a bench, but this time while at an incline angle. Remember to squeeze the shoulder blades together to get a good "set" position. Ideally, hand placement on the bar should be at a width between your bench press and overhead press width. Find what's comfortable for you but, again, do not roll the thumbs behind the bar – keep them wrapped around the bar, which is a good rule to follow for any pressing motion.

STRICT OVERHEAD PRESS (OHP): This overhead press is to be done while standing. With the bar set within a power rack at the height of your squat, take the bar out of the cups and back into position. Your hand placement on the bar should be narrower than your bench press or incline press. I like to have my hands about a thumbs length inside of where my I grip for bench press. Press the bar over your head with knees locked in place. This is not a push press or jerk – your knees should not bend nor should you "drop" under the bar. This is a strict press for proper development and power transfer overhead. As you are pressing, work to "push" your head through the window, or box, that your arms have created for you overhead. This will help you in locking out your press. Push into and through the bar, not away. Too many people arch way back, greatly adjusting the angle at which you are pressing. Once pressed, return the bar to the starting point, which should be in line with your collarbone. Don't stop the bar at your chin or nose – you'll hear some people state that they do that for shoulder health. It's a lie. It's easier with less range of motion, so please; don't shortchange yourself in an attempt to increase your working sets by five or 10 pounds.

SEATED "Z" PRESS: Sit inside a power rack with the bar being held by the crash/spotter bars. The bar should sit about collarbone height, or close. Overhead press the bar, focusing on pushing your head through the "hole" your arms created for you upon pressing. Return the bar to the start position, but do not touch the crash bars. There's nothing wrong with the bar coming below chin level. Please, I'd prefer you touch your chest with it then stop it at or above the chin level. Hand width should be set about the same as your standing overhead press (shoulder width, with the thumbs around the bar).

3-WAY SHOULDER RAISES: Taking dumbbells, raise them to the front for the desired reps, then the side, then the back. Specific order is not critical.

REAR DELT/FLY: Lie backwards on an incline bench with your face in the place where normally the back of your head would be. With dumbbells in your hands, pull the weights up and out to your side – squeeze your shoulder blades as you perform a "fly," only facing the opposite direction. Your palms should be pointed down, ideally, but hand placement is not a high priority. You can also perform this exercise with a band while standing up or while flipped backwards on a pec deck. Focus, again, on squeezing your shoulder blades together.

SHRUGS: Load the barbell up with substantially more weight than you hang clean. This exercise is best done inside a power rack with the bar, in the rested position, at mid-quad height. Use an overhand grip with lifting straps. To perform the exercise, concentrate on pushing your shoulders up to your ear lobes. Do not rotate the shoulders front to back and vice versa. This is a great lift to overload your shoulders and prepare your body for the heavier cleans of the future. It sounds odd, but when I am doing shrugs on a consistent basis, my hang cleans improve. Commit to a full cycle of doing this exercise and see for yourself.

12

TRUE VICTORY

As great as it is to turn a monster caber, hit the game winning homerun, cause a fumble or clear a PR in weight over bar, there's a more amazing feeling. It's a feeling of victory ... true victory. This victory is eternal life through Jesus Christ.

Attaining true victory can be found through the ABC's. Yep, it's that simple.

A-ADMIT
First, you must admit that you're a sinner, or gone against God's will. Romans 3:23 says, "for all have sinned and fall short of the glory of God." We've all sinned, no one (except Jesus) has lived a perfect life. Because of this, we can't make it to heaven, and deserve to spend eternity in hell. We have to ADMIT that we can't make it alone. ADMIT that you need Jesus.

B-BELIEVE
Next, you must believe that Jesus died on the cross for everyone. "For God so loved the world, that he sent his one and only Son, that whosoever believes in Him will not perish, but have everlasting life." John 3:16. He loved each and every one of us so much, that He died and rose again so that we might live forever in heaven. BELIEVE that Jesus died and rose from the dead for you.

C-COMMIT
Lastly, you must commit your life to Jesus. Romans 10:9 says, "That if you confess with your mouth, Jesus is Lord, and believe in your heart that God raised Him from the dead, you will be saved." Pray and ask Him to come and live in your heart. You cannot make it into heaven on your own, but by committing your life to Jesus and asking Him to save you from your sin, you can spend eternity with Him. If you'd like to ask Him into your heart, simply pray something like this:

> *Jesus, I know I've sinned, and I'm sorry. Please forgive me and come into my heart. Take control of my life. I know only You can save me, and I commit my life to you. Amen.*

If you just prayed that prayer for the first time, you've just make the most important decision in your life! Please, let me know if you have made this amazing decision ... **you've now attained true victory!**

sinews

BEHEMOTH

WEEKS 1 & 2

MONDAY
Bench 3x12
Cl Grip Bench 3x12
Dips 3xmax#
Push Ups 3xmax#
Flys 3x12
Tris 3x12 - choose two
Abs/Core - choose two

TUESDAY
Rack Clean 3x5
Back Squat 3x12
RDL 3x12
Gluteham 3x12
Hip Thrusters 3x12

WEDNESDAY
Lat Pulls 3x12
Pull ups 3xmax#
Seated rows 3x12
Inverted Pull Ups 3x12
Chest Supported Rows 3x12
Bis 3x12 - choose two
Abs/Core - choose two

THURSDAY
Incline 3x12
Strict OH Press 3x12
"Z" Press 3x12
Rear delt/fly 3x12
DB raise - 3-way 3x12
Shrugs 3x15

FRIDAY
Rack Snatch 3x5
Front Squat 3x12
Step Ups 3x8 ea
Backwards Staircase/Hill 3xmax
Lunges 3x12 ea
Abs/Core - choose two

sinews

BEHEMOTH

WEEKS 3 & 4

MONDAY
- Bench 3x10
- Cl Grip Bench 3x10 (add bands)
- Dips 3xmax# (add resistance)
- Pull Over and Press 3x10
- Flys 3x10
- Tris 3x10 - choose two
- Abs/Core - choose two

TUESDAY
- Hang Clean 3x5
- Back Squat 3x10
- Gluteham 3x10
- Straight Leg Dead 3x10
- Leg Curls/Hip Thrusters 3x10

WEDNESDAY
- Lat Pulls 3x10
- Pull ups 3xmax#
- Seated rows 3x10
- Chest Supported Rows 3x10
- Low Rows 3x10
- Bis 3x10 - choose two
- Abs/Core - choose two

THURSDAY
- Strict OH Press 3x10
- Incline 3x10
- "Z" Press 3x10
- Rear delt/fly 3x10
- DB raise - 3-way 3x10
- Shrugs 3x10

FRIDAY
- Hang Snatch 3x5
- Front Squat 3x10
- Step Ups 3x8 ea
- Backwards Weighted Sled Drag 3xmax
- Single Leg Squat 3x10 ea.
- Abs/Core - choose two

BEHEMOTH

rest

WEEK 5

bronze

WEEKS 6 & 7

MONDAY
Bench 4x6
Cl Grip Bench 4x6
Dips 3xmax#
Push Ups 3xmax#
Flys 3x8
Tris 3x6 - choose two
Abs/Core - choose two

TUESDAY
Hang Cleans 4x4
Back Squat 4x6
Gluteham 3x8
RDL 3x8
Leg Curls/Hip Thr 3x6 single leg

WEDNESDAY
Lat Pulls 3x6
Pull ups 3xmax#
Seated rows 3x6
Inverted Pull Ups 3x6 w/wt
DB Rows 3x6
Bis 3x6 - choose two
Abs/Core - choose two

THURSDAY
Incline 4x6
Strict OH Press 4x6
Z Press 4x6
Rear delt/fly 3x8
One arm OH Press 4x6 ea.
Shrugs 4x6

FRIDAY
Hang Snatch 4x4
Front Squat 4x6
One-leg squat 4x6 ea.
Backwards sled drag 4xmax
Diamond Bar Jumps 4x6
Abs/Core - choose two

bronze

BENCH/BENCH

WEEKS 8 & 9

MONDAY
Bench 5,5,3,3
Cl Grip Bench 5,5,3,3 (banded)
Dips 3x6 w/ wt
Pull over and press 3x5
Flys 3x8
Tris 3x6 - choose two
Abs/Core - choose two

TUESDAY
Hang Cleans 3x3
Back Squat 5,5,3,3
RDL 3x5
Gluteham 3x8
Banded Str Leg Deads 3x8 w/ wt or band
Leg Curls/Hip Thr 3x6 single leg

WEDNESDAY
Lat Pulls 4x5
Pull ups 3x6 w/wt
DB Rows 3x5
Inverted Pull Ups 3x5 w/wt
Seated Rows 3x5
Bis 3x6 - choose two
Abs/Core - choose two

THURSDAY
Incline 5,5,3,3
Strict OH Press 5,5,3,3
Z Press 4x6
Rear delt/fly 3x6
Side/Front DB raise 3x6 ea.
Shrugs 4x6

FRIDAY
Hang Snatch 3x3
Front Squat 5,5,3,3
Step Ups 3x4 ea.
Backwards sled drag 4xmax
Lunges 3x5 ea.
Abs/Core - choose two

iron

WEEKS 11 & 12

MONDAY
Bench 3x3
Cl Grip Bench 3x3 (banded)
Dips 3x5 w/ wt
Pull over and press 3x5
Flys 3x8
Tris 3x5 - choose two
Abs/Core - choose two

TUESDAY
Hang Cleans 2,2,2
Back Squat 3x3
Gluteham 3x6 w/wt or band
Banded Str Leg Deads 3x8
Hip Thrusters 3x5 HEAVY

WEDNESDAY
Lat Pulls 4x5
Pull ups 3x5 w/wt
DB Rows 3x5
Inverted Pull Ups 3x5 w/wt
Seated Rows 3x5
Bis 3x5 - choose two
Abs/Core - choose two

THURSDAY
Incline 3x3
Strict OH Press 3x3
Z Press 3x5
Rear delt/fly 3x6
Side/Front DB raise 3x6 ea.
Shrugs 4x6 HEAVY

FRIDAY
Hang Snatch 2,2,2
Front Squat 3x3
Step Ups 3x3 ea. HEAVY
One leg squat 3x5 ea.
Banded Knee Ext. 3x10 ea.
Abs/Core - choose two

iron

WEEK 13

MONDAY
Bench 3,2,2,2
Cl Grip Bench 3,2,2,2 (banded)
Dips 3x5 w/ wt
Pull over and press 3x5
Flys 3x8
Tris 3x5 - choose two
Abs/Core - choose two

TUESDAY
Hang Cleans 2,1,1,1
Back Squat 3,2,2,2
Gluteham 3x5 w/wt or band
Banded Str Leg Deads 3x8
RDL 3x3
Leg curls 3x8

WEDNESDAY
Lat Pulls 3x4
Pull ups 3x3 w/wt
DB Rows 3x5
Inverted Pull Ups 3x3 w/wt
Seated Rows 3x5
Bis 3x5 - choose two
Abs/Core - choose two

THURSDAY
Incline 3,2,2,2
Strict OH Press 3,2,2,2
Z Press 3x3
Rear delt/fly 3x6
Side/Front DB raise 3x6 ea.
Shrugs 4x6 HEAVY

FRIDAY
Hang Snatch 2,1,1,1
Front Squat 3,2,2,2
Step Ups 3x3 ea.
Backwards sled drag 3xmax
Diamond Bar Jumps 3x3
One leg squat 3x5 ea.

BEHEMOTH

test

WEEK 14

MONDAY
Bench
Cl Grip Bench

TUESDAY
Hang Cleans
Back Squats

WEDNESDAY
Off

THURSDAY
Incline
Strict OH Press

FRIDAY
Hang Snatch
Front Squat

Made in the USA
San Bernardino, CA
11 June 2014